LEWIS & CLARK

Path to the Pacific

★ ★ ★

Jana Eisenberg

Children's Press®
A Division of Scholastic Inc.
New York / Toronto / London / Auckland / Sydney
Mexico City / New Delhi / Hong Kong
Danbury, Connecticut

Book Design: Mindy Liu and Mikhail Bortnik
Contributing Editor: Kevin Somers
Photo Credits: Cover, pp. 4, 18 © Bettman/Corbis; p. 8 © Index Stock Imagery, Inc.; p. 13 © North Wind Picture Archives; p. 14 © Macduff Everton/Corbis; pp. 16, 26, 29, 34 © Connie Ricca/Corbis; p. 17 Yale Collection of Western Americana, Beinecke Rare Book and Manuscript Library; p. 23 © Corbis; p. 25 © Getty Images; p. 33 © McCormick Library of Special Collections, Northwestern University Library; p. 39 © U.S. Mint Handout/Reuters/Corbis; p. 41 © David Muench/Corbis

Library of Congress Cataloging-in-Publication Data

Eisenberg, Jana.
  Lewis and Clark : path to the Pacific / Jana Eisenberg.
  p. cm. — (Trailblazers of the West)
  Includes bibliographical references and index.
  ISBN 0-516-25126-0 (lib. bdg) — ISBN 0-516-25096-5 (pbk.)
  1. Lewis and Clark Expedition (1804–1806)—Juvenile literature. 2. West (U.S.)—Discovery and exploration—Juvenile literature. 3. West (U.S.)—Description and travel—Juvenile literature. I. Title. II. Series.

F592.7.E425 2005
917.804'2—dc22
                                        2005002695

CONTENTS

INTRODUCTION

On April 30, 1803, the United States doubled its size with the simple stroke of a pen. On that day, the United States and France signed a treaty known as the Louisiana Purchase. For the price of three cents an acre, the United States bought from France the land that stretched from New Orleans to Canada, and from the Mississippi River to what is now Colorado and Idaho.

But the United States did not know exactly what they were buying. All of these western lands were unknown to the white people living in the United States. Now these new lands would have to be explored. Someone had to see what this new half of America looked like. Who would be up for such a huge challenge?

By signing the Louisiana Purchase, Thomas Jefferson set the stage for the future growth of America.

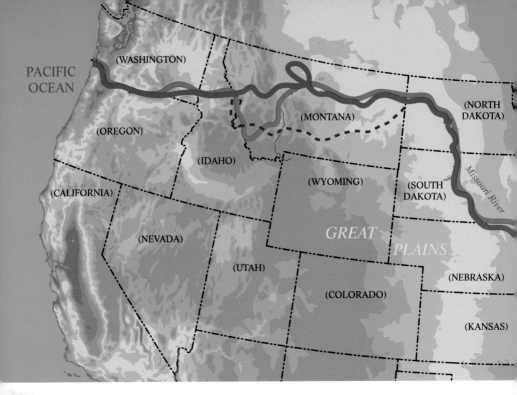

President Thomas Jefferson thought that
Meriwether Lewis and William Clark were
the right men for the job. Jefferson appointed
Lewis and Clark to lead an expedition to
explore America's new territories. Lewis and
Clark brought together a group of about four
dozen of the most skilled men from all
corners of the young nation. This group was
called the Corps of Discovery.

Lewis and Clark had prepared and studied
for this journey for years. Still, the expedition
would not be easy. There were almost no
maps of this area at the time. There were not
many roads in the area either. Getting supplies

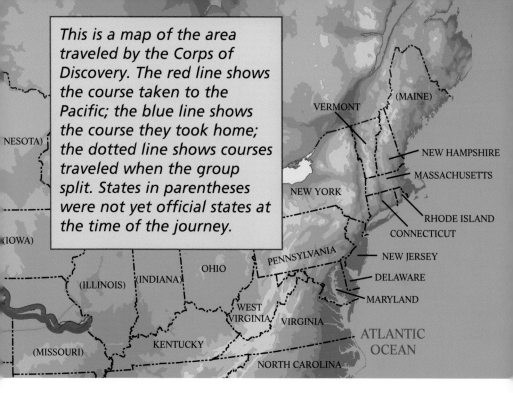

This is a map of the area traveled by the Corps of Discovery. The red line shows the course taken to the Pacific; the blue line shows the course they took home; the dotted line shows courses traveled when the group split. States in parentheses were not yet official states at the time of the journey.

and food would get harder as the trip took the Corps deeper into unexplored lands.

There were other problems to face. Many tribes of Native Americans lived in these areas. The Corps of Discovery would need help from as many of these people as possible. However, there would be language and cultural differences to overcome. The possibility of fighting with Native Americans would also be a constant concern. The Corps of Discovery were about to face many obstacles and to risk the many dangers of the unknown. The odds of them returning alive seemed slim.

CHAPTER 1

GETTING READY

A New Nation Grows

Even before the United States owned the Louisiana territory, President Jefferson had his heart set on exploring these lands. He had already decided that his personal secretary, Meriwether Lewis, would lead this important journey. Lewis was twenty-six years old when President Jefferson hired him as a private secretary. Jefferson sent Lewis to study with special teachers to get ready for the journey. Lewis learned about natural history, astronomy, and botany, or the study of plants. Lewis would be responsible for keeping careful notes.

As they prepared for the journey, Jefferson realized that Lewis would need a co-commander. Lewis chose fellow Virginian William Clark as his partner. Clark had made a strong impression on Lewis while they were in the army together.

Lewis and Clark were very fair leaders. They allowed their men to have a say in major decisions and they showed no cruelty in their punishment for bad behavior.

A GROWING NATION

By 1803, England's powerful navy controlled the seas. England's control of the waterways made it difficult for France to oversee the land it owned in North America. The Louisiana territory was part of those oversea lands that France owned. Napoleon Bonaparte, the emperor of France, decided to sell this land.

America paid fifteen million dollars for more then 800,000 square miles (2.1 million square kilometers) of the Louisiana territory. The Louisiana Purchase made the United States one of the largest nations in the world. This area of land would later become the states of Louisiana, Arkansas, Oklahoma, Missouri, Kansas, Nebraska, Iowa, South Dakota, Wyoming, Minnesota, Colorado, North Dakota, and Montana.

The Assignment
Jefferson gave Lewis and Clark a list of things to get done on their trip. One was to see if they could discover a new water route to reach the Pacific Ocean. If a water route to the Pacific was discovered, trading opportunities with Asia would be possible. Many people at this time believed such a route existed. They called it the Northwest Passage. President Jefferson believed the discovery of the Northwest Passage would greatly increase the wealth of America.

Making Friends
Jefferson also wanted Lewis and Clark to meet with Native Americans. Jefferson had studied all he could about native languages and ways of life. But his knowledge was limited to the Native Americans who lived in the eastern parts of America. He was curious to learn about the Native people to the west. Jefferson also hoped that if these Indians were befriended, they could be convinced to trade with America instead of with the British.

★ FRONTIER FACT ★

One of the best ways the members of the Corps of Discovery befriended Native Americans was through song and dance. Pierre Cruzatte was a member of the Corps who was able to use his talent as a fiddle player to do this.

Jefferson also wanted Lewis and Clark to return with accurate information about the plants, animals, and land that were part of the new territory. At the time, there were myths and stories about these lands. Many people even believed that these areas were filled with giant woolly mammoths that roamed free.

A Strong Team

Lewis and Clark were an excellent team to lead this mission. They had both trained as military leaders. They could inspire people to work hard and could keep up the team's spirits. Lewis was a skilled naturalist capable of identifying and recording scientific finds. He also knew about the science of astronomy.

Using astronomy, he could tell directions by looking at the stars. This would help the group stay on course throughout their journey. Clark was a talented mapmaker. By the end of the expedition he had made some of the best, earliest maps of the area. But their first task as leaders was to choose members for their expedition.

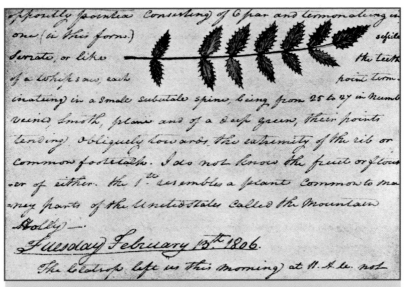

Lewis and Clark recorded many scientific discoveries on their journey. Clark's sketch of an evergreen shrub leaf appears on this page from his journal.

Lewis and Clark began assembling their team in 1803. They chose men with many different kinds of skills. They included men from the army, such as John Ordway, John Colter, and Patrick Gass. These men had battle skills and were used to living in rough conditions. John Shields, another army man, was a blacksmith. George Drouillard was not from the army but his father was French-Canadian and his mother was a Shawnee Indian. He was an excellent woodsman. He also spoke different Native American languages. Pierre Cruzatte and François Labiche were excellent boatsmen. The group even had a mascot. Before leaving, Captain Lewis bought a Newfoundland dog. Lewis

This actor is playing George Drouillard at a Lewis and Clark festival. He holds lead balls that were used in guns from that era.

named the dog Seaman. Seaman made the entire journey with his master and the group.

Pitching In and Setting Off

In December 1803, the Corps of Discovery and their leaders gathered at a place they later named Camp River Dubois, which they also called Camp Wood. It was located in what is present-day Illinois, near the Mississippi and Missouri rivers. They built a campsite with cabins. This camp was a military camp, so the men were required to train and uphold military regulations. They spent one winter there, learning to work together. Lewis and Clark began their weather diaries and astronomical observations at this time. They kept these diaries throughout their journey.

The Corps of Discovery kept busy at Camp Wood. There, Captain Lewis learned new information about the Missouri River, from its mouth to the Mandan Indian villages in present-day North Dakota. He also invented a

This is a replica of the keelboat Discovery. *The keelboat is on display at the Lewis and Clark State Park in Iowa.*

new kind of boat called a keelboat. This boat was designed to travel in shallow river waters yet it could carry about 12 tons (10.9 metric tons) of cargo. The group also made changes to their other boats to better suit them for the trip. Food and other supplies were packed. These supplies included gifts for the Native American leaders they would encounter.

Finally, on May 14, 1804, Lewis, Clark, and about forty men started out on their bold adventure west.

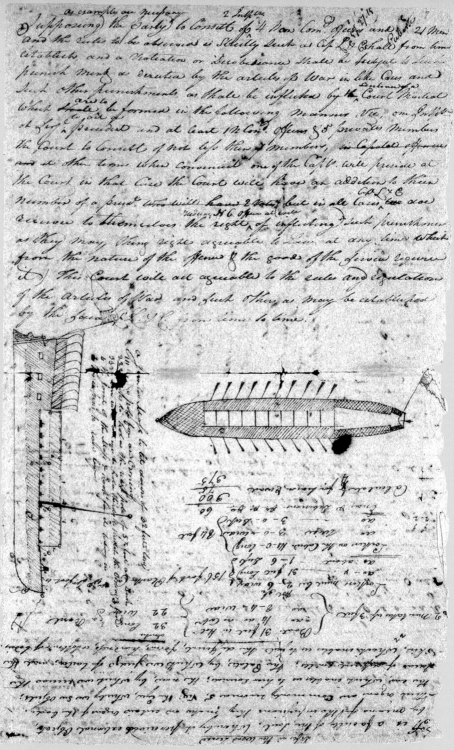

This is a page from Captain Clark's field notes. Among his notes are drawings of the keelboat Discovery.

CHAPTER 2

WESTWARD HO!

In August 1804, north of present-day Omaha, Nebraska, Lewis and Clark had their first official meeting with Native Americans. They met with leaders of the Oto and Missouri people to deliver a message from President Jefferson. First they gave the chiefs peace medals, fifteen-star flags, and other gifts. Then they showed the Indians items such as compasses and telescopes. They also spoke about President Jefferson. They called him the "great father" far to the east. The captains promised a future of peace and prosperity if tribes did not make war on whites or other Native American tribes.

Less than four months after the Corps of Discovery set out from Camp Wood, they were hit with their first major tragedy. Near what is now Sioux City, Iowa, Sergeant

Over the course of the expedition the captains would meet with many groups of Native Americans, offering them gifts of friendship whenever they could.

Charles Floyd became very ill. On August 20, 1804, he died from what may have been a burst appendix. In his journal William Clark wrote, "Floyd Died with a great deal of composure, before his death he said to me, I am going away I want you to write me a letter." Lewis and Clark honored Floyd by naming the hilltop where they buried him Floyd's Bluff. Sergeant Floyd was the first U.S. soldier to die west of the Mississippi River.

Discovering Wildlife

As the group moved through the Great Plains, they recorded information about the animals they saw, such as antelope, mule deer, and coyotes. These animals were completely unknown in the East. In total, Lewis and Clark would describe in their journals 178 plants and 122 animals that had not yet been recorded. On September 7, 1804, the Corps discovered prairie dogs. The group was fascinated by this animal. They captured one to send back to President Jefferson.

MEETING WITH THE NATIVE AMERICANS

The Corps of Discovery met close to fifty different Native American people in the course of their travels. Among these groups were the Otos, Missouris, Teton Sioux, Mandans, Shoshones, and Blackfeet.

Most of the Corps's encounters with the tribes went well. Friendships with Indians were very important to the success of the expedition. In fact, the group would not have survived the journey without the help of Native Americans. They were saved from starvation by the kindness of tribes such as the Nez Percé. These people were so kind to the Corps that Lewis called them, in his own words, "the most hospitable, honest and sincere people that we have met with in our voyage."

★FRONTIER FACT★

Lewis and Clark and their men had heard tales of fierce grizzly bears. The first grizzly they ran into weighed about 300 pounds (136 kilograms). They had no trouble killing it. About two days later, they met a much larger grizzly that weighed over 500 pounds (227 kg). The men shot it about eight or nine times. This only seemed to anger the animal, and it chased them away!

In October 1804, after traveling about 1,600 miles (2,575 kilometers), the Corps of Discovery reached the villages of the Mandans and Hidatsas people. This was north of what is now Bismarck, North Dakota. About 4,500 people lived there, a very large population at the time. In fact, more people lived there than in the country's capital, Washington, D.C. These people were friendly toward the Corps. Lewis and Clark decided to build their first winter camp there. While at this camp, the Corps met a French-Canadian trader named Toussaint Charbonneau and his wife, Sacagawea. She was a Shoshone Indian who

Patrick Gass created this drawing of Captain Clark with a group of men from the Corps hunting bears.

was about fifteen years old. The captains believed the two could be helpful when the expedition reached the mountains farther west. They brought them along as interpreters and guides.

By late December, the temperature had dropped to -45° Fahrenheit (-7° Celsius). The group had never experienced weather this cold. During this harsh winter, Mandan men and several men from the expedition hunted buffalo together. Several expedition members and a Mandan boy got frostbite. Lewis would later have to remove the boy's toes, without any painkillers.

In February 1805, Sacagawea went into labor. Lewis notes in his journal that her labor was long and painful. In an attempt to speed up her child's birth, a medicine made from a rattlesnake's rattle was given to Sacagawea. Captain Lewis was doubtful of the medicine's effectiveness, although it seemed to work. Ten minutes after she took the medicine, Sacagawea gave birth to a baby boy, Jean Baptiste.

Sacagawea was more than an interpreter. She was a valued member of the crew. At one point during the journey there was a boat accident. While other crew members were panicking, she calmly plucked journals, medicines, and other supplies from the freezing water after they washed overboard.

CHAPTER 3

DIFFICULT TIMES

On April 7, 1805, the Corps set off from their winter camp. Lewis and Clark sent the keelboat with thirteen men down the Missouri River. The keelboat was loaded with maps, reports, Indian artifacts, and boxes of scientific and other discoveries for President Jefferson. Among these discoveries were five live animals, including the prairie dog.

The rest of the Corps headed west on the Missouri River. They were traveling in two pirogues and six smaller canoes. As they pressed on, Captain Lewis wrote, "We were now about to penetrate a country at least two thousand miles in width, on which the foot of civilized man had never trodden."

This is one of the canoes used by the Corps of Discovery. It is called a dugout canoe because it is made from hollowing out the center of a log.

At one point in their journey, Clark's men were having trouble sleeping. The reason? Their route had taken them very near to giant herds of buffalo. The animals' grunting and snorting kept them awake at night!

In early June, the expedition traveling west came to a fork in the river. The crew believed they should take the north fork of the Missouri. Lewis and Clark thought they should take the south fork. Even though the crew thought their way was right, they agreed to take the south fork. According to Meriwether Lewis, "They were ready to follow us anywhere we thought proper to direct." According to what the Hidatsas had told them, they would soon come across a large waterfall if they were on the right course.

Later in June, the expedition reached the Great Falls of the Missouri, proof that Lewis and Clark had chosen the right path. Then they unexpectedly discovered four more waterfalls a short way upriver. They had to carry their boats on land, 18.5 miles (22 km) to get around the falls. This would prove to be a difficult task. Sometimes it was so windy that they couldn't move at all. Mosquitoes and gnats constantly stung the men. Sharp plants on the ground hurt their feet as they moved their heavy loads. Rainstorms forced them to stop. It would take them nearly a month to get beyond the falls.

Lewis and Clark had planned on taking less than one day to go around the Great Falls of the Missouri River. However, the falls turned out to be much greater than the group had expected and the task took close to a month.

On August 12, 1805, President Jefferson received the shipment that was sent to him after the Corps left the Mandan village in April. In the shipment was a letter from Lewis. From the hopeful estimate Lewis gave the president, Jefferson believed the group would have reached the Pacific Ocean by the time he read the letter. But in reality, Lewis was only at Lemhi Pass, on the present-day border between Montana and Idaho. From this viewpoint, Lewis had expected to see a vast plain running west with a large river flowing to the Pacific. He believed the Northwest Passage continued beyond this point. Instead, all he saw was more mountains.

Fortunes and Misfortunes

In late August 1805, the Corps met the Shoshone people. Fortunately, the chief of the Shoshone was Sacagawea's brother. The Corps were provided with twenty-nine fresh horses, a mule, and a guide named Old Toby.

BABY ON BOARD

Toussaint Charbonneau and Sacagawea were very helpful to the Lewis and Clark expedition. Sacagawea came from the Shoshone tribe of Native Americans. Because she was a Native American woman on such an important trip with white men, she became as famous as Lewis and Clark.

Charbonneau and Sacagawea's child, Jean Baptiste Charbonneau, nicknamed Little Pomp, was born during the expedition. Having a baby along on the journey made it seem like a family. This was helpful when they met certain groups of Native Americans. These Native American groups believed the expedition must be a peaceful one if they traveled with a baby.

On September 11, the group climbed into the Bitterroot Mountains. Sergeant Patrick Gass called them "the most terrible mountains I ever beheld." Old Toby lost the trail in the steep and heavily wooded mountains. Then the explorers ran short of food. It also started to snow, just as the group realized that the mountains went on farther than they expected.

By late September 1805, the starving Corps made it to the homeland of the Nez Percé. The Nez Percé befriended them and fed them. A chief named Twisted Hair helped them make new canoes. The group pushed on traveling from the Clearwater River to the Snake River. From there they reached the Columbia River, headed for the Pacific Ocean.

Looks Like We Made It!

By November 1805, the Corps had made it to the Pacific Ocean. They were happy, although their journey was not over. Now they had to think about the trip back. The weather was horrible, and they could not decide what to

This man is a member of the Nez Percé tribe. These generous people saved the Corps from starvation as they stumbled out of the Bitterroot Mountains in the autumn of 1805.

do. Would they stay for the winter? Should they start back right away? Finally, they took a vote. The group decided to stay for the rest of the winter near a group of Clatsop Indians. In December 1805, they selected their campsite. They built their last fort. Lewis and Clark correctly guessed that they had traveled over 4,000 miles (6,440 km).

CHAPTER 4

HEADING BACK EAST

In March 1806, it was time to head home.
Soon after they started out, they met up with
Walula Indians. It was April, almost
springtime. The chief of the tribe told them
that traveling would be hard or impossible
because of bad weather conditions. But on
June 14, 1806, they left anyway. This was a
mistake. They soon realized the snow was too
deep to push ahead. For the first time on their
long journey they had to turn back. On June
24, they started out again with Native
American guides.

Breaking Up the Party

In July 1806, Lewis and Clark split up the
group for part of the return trip. Lewis took
a small group to explore the northernmost
reaches of the Marias River. Clark would
lead the remaining men down the
Yellowstone River.

*After spending an extremely rainy winter at Fort
Clatsop (replica shown), the homesick Corps began its
journey back east on March 23, 1806.*

★FRONTIER FACT★

Pierre Cruzatte, the fiddler and boatsman, had bad eyesight. On August 11, 1806, while they were out hunting, he accidentally shot Captain Lewis in the thigh!

During Lewis's part of that journey, he and his men met and fought with some members of the Blackfeet tribe. Two Blackfeet men were killed. This was the only reported case of Native Americans dying because of a fight with the members of the Corps of Discovery.

On August 12, 1806, Lewis and his crew reunited with Clark and the rest of the Corps downstream from the mouth of the Yellowstone River. Having been gone nearly two-and-a-half years, the rest of America had given them up for dead. On September 23, 1806, the Corps of Discovery arrived in St. Louis and were warmly greeted by surprised citizens.

FIRST NEWS OF THEIR RETURN

Clark's journal reports that on September 17, 1806, while on the final leg of their journey down the Kansas River, they met a Captain McLellan. The captain was "astonished" to see them return. Clark and his men got news about politics from the captain. They also accepted gifts, which included chocolate and whisky, and continued their homeward trip.

After the Journey

Returning to normal life, Lewis was named governor of Louisiana. Being governor did not come as easily to him as being a captain. He ran into financial problems and struggled with debt. He also had a difficult time organizing his journals for publication. He suffered from severe emotional health problems. Meriwether Lewis took his own life in October 1809.

Clark had been appointed as a federal agent of Indian affairs. He was successful and well liked. After Lewis died, Clark took over getting the journals ready. He married and had several children, one of whom he named Meriwether Lewis Clark. William Clark lived until 1838.

Lewis and Clark Remembered

Today there are millions of words written about every detail of their journey. Every year, new books and studies come out, exploring the facts about Lewis and Clark's trip.

All over the United States there are monuments and statues named after Lewis and Clark. There are schools, towns, trails, mountains, and rivers named after them. In August 2004, the United States even put them on the new nickel! Thomas Jefferson is on the front and Lewis and Clark's keelboat is on the back.

In 2004, the image of either the keelboat Discovery *or the Peace Medal was put on the reverse side of the nickel as part of the Westward Journey Nickel Series.*

Who Were Those Guys?

Lewis and Clark's accomplishments were and still are impressive. In two-and-a-half years they traveled over 8,000 miles (12,875 km). They led a large and slow-moving group through many dangers and hardships. The tight-knit group stayed in harmony the whole time. Fortunately, they lost only one man on the expedition, and he died of natural causes.

Lewis and Clark explored and mapped land and rivers that had never been seen by white people. They met and talked to many Native American people. Lewis and Clark built many trade relationships with these people. This led to increased American interest in the fur trade and in the commercial development of the West.

They saw, wrote about, and brought back samples of hundreds of species of then-unknown plant and animal life. In all, they recorded for science more than 120 animal species and over 175 plant species. Lewis and Clark also added to geographic knowledge by making maps of the areas they visited. Although they proved that the Northwest Passage didn't exist, they proved the success of overland travel to the Pacific.

Their Legend Lives

Today, most people know the names Meriwether Lewis and William Clark. They were brave and resourceful men. They took on and accomplished a fantastic journey. No one even dreamed just how important it would turn out to be. The spirit of their trip has come to stand for the dreams of America's West.

Each year, people visit the many sites of Lewis and Clark's journey. Lewis and Clark stopped at this point of South Dakota's White River in September 1804. ▶

accurate (ak-yuh-ruht) exactly correct

appendix (uh-**pen**-diks) a small, closed tube leading from the large intestine

astronomy (uh-**stron**-uh-mee) the study of stars, planets, and space

composure (kuhm-poh-zhur) a calm state; self-control

corps (cor) a group of people acting together

cultural (kuhl-chur-uhl) having to do with the way of life, ideas, customs, and traditions of a group of people

diary (dye-uh-ree) a book in which people write down things that happen each day, either to use as a record or to plan ahead

expedition (ek-spuh-**dish**-uhn) A long journey for a special purpose, such as exploring

explore (ek-splor) to travel in order to discover what a place is like

frostbite (**frawst**-bite) when parts of the body, such as fingers, toes, or ears, are damaged by extreme cold

geographic (jee-o-**gra**-fik) to do with the study of the earth, including its people, resources, climate, and physical features

harmony (**har**-muh-nee) agreement, working together

interpreter (in-**tur**-prit-er) someone who translates a language for someone else

keelboat (**keel**-bote) a shallow riverboat that is rowed, pushed by pole, or towed

naturalist (**nach**-er-uh-list) someone who specializes in the study of plants and animals

pirogue (**pe**-rog) a canoelike boat

prosperity (**pross**-per-uh-tee) the condition of being successful or thriving

regulations (reg-yuh-**lay**-shuhnz) official rules or orders

FOR FURTHER READING

Ambrose, Stephen. *Undaunted Courage: Meriwether Lewis, Thomas Jefferson and the Opening of the American West*. New York: Simon & Schuster, 1997.

Bowen, Andy Russell. *The Back of Beyond: A Story about Lewis and Clark*. Minneapolis, MN: Carolrhoda Books, Inc., 1998.

Bruchac, Joseph. *Sacajawea*. New York: Scholastic Inc., 2001.

Hinshaw Patent, Dorothy. *Animals on the Trail with Lewis and Clark*. Boston: Clarion Books, 2002.

Roop, Peter. *Off the Map: The Journals of Lewis and Clark*. New York: Walker & Company, 1998.

Organizations

Lewis and Clark Center
701 Riverside Dr.
St. Charles, MO 63301
(636)-947-3199
www.lewisandclarktrail.com/section1/mocities/
St.Charles/L&Ccenter/

Lewis and Clark National Historic Trail
Interpretive Center
4201 Giant Springs Rd.
P.O. Box 1806
Great Falls, MT 59403-1806
(406)-727-8733

The Museum of Westward Expansion
The Gateway Arch Riverfront
St. Louis Riverfront
St. Louis, MO 63102
(877)-982-1410
www. info@gatewayarch.com

RESOURCES

Web Sites

Lewis and Clark: Mapping the West
www.edgate.com/lewisandclark
This site from the Smithsonian Museum provides a virtual exhibit of Lewis and Clark, including a variety of maps and lesson plans.

Lewis and Clark State Historical Site
www.campdubois.com/history.html
Learn more about the camp where the Corps of Discovery was trained before setting out on their magnificent journey. See what exhibits are on display at Camp River Dubois.

National Geographic: Lewis and Clark
www.nationalgeographic.com/lewisandclark
This site clearly presents lists of the expedition's discoveries and equipment, as well as a time line. Check out the wonderful photo gallery or take an interactive journey with Lewis and Clark.

INDEX

About the Author

Jana Eisenberg is a freelance writer who lives in Buffalo, New York, with her husband.